CREATURES OF THE PARANORMAL

AMERICAN VAMPIRES

Linda R. Baker

I0889211

Enslow Publishing
101 W. 23rd Street
Suite 240
New York, NY 10011
USA
enslow.com

Published in 2020 by Enslow Publishing, LLC
101 W. 23rd Street, Suite 240, New York, NY 10011

Copyright © 2020 by Enslow Publishing, LLC

All rights reserved.

No part of this book may be reproduced by any means without the written permission of the publisher.

Library of Congress Cataloging-in-Publication Data

Names: Baker, Linda R., author.
Title: American vampires / Linda R. Baker.
Description: New York : Enslow Publishing, 2020 | Series: Creatures of the paranormal | Audience: Grades: 5-8. | Includes bibliographical references and index.
Identifiers: LCCN 2019011994| ISBN 9781978513600 (library bound) | ISBN 9781978513594 (pbk.)
Subjects: LCSH: Vampires—United States—Juvenile literature.
Classification: LCC GR830.V3 B335 2020 | DDC 398.21—dc23
LC record available at https://lccn.loc.gov/2019011994

Printed in the United States of America

To Our Readers: We have done our best to make sure all websites in this book were active and appropriate when we went to press. However, the author and the publisher have no control over and assume no liability for the material available on those websites or on any websites they may link to. Any comments or suggestions can be sent by email to customerservice@enslow.com.

Portions of this book originally appeared in *Vampires in America* by Sam Navarre.

Photo Credits: Cover and p. 1 (top) Stocksnapper/Shutterstock.com; cover and p. 1 (bottom) D-Keine/E+/Getty Images; p. 5 Werner Forman/Universal Images Group/ Getty Images; p. 6 Stock Montage/Archive Photos/ Getty Images; p. 10 Christophel Fine Art/ Universal Images Group/ Getty Images; p. 13 Nikolay Doychinov/AFP/GettyImages; p. 15 Wikimedia Commons/ File: Believe in Vampires.png/Public Domain; p. 19 Michael Lynch/ Shutterstock.com; p. 21 patrimonio designs ltd/ Shutterstock.com; p. 23 Jim West / Alamy Stock Photo; p. 27 Hulton Archive/ Getty Images; p. 31 Silver Screen Collection /Moviepix/ Getty Images; pp. 32, 39 AF archive / Alamy Stock Photo; p. 35 Warner Bros. / Moviepix/ Getty Images; p. 37 PictureLux / The Hollywood Archive / Alamy Stock Photo; p. 40 Anna Calypso/ Shutterstock.com.

CONTENTS

INTRODUCTION

What is a vampire? The most common definition is an undead human who must drink blood in order to survive and will be set ablaze or, at best, weakened by sunlight. Vampires were not always referred to as vampires in folklore. "Reanimated corpses" as a description of vampires first appeared in 1810 according to author Katherine Ramsland. The most well-known vampire first appeared in print in Bram Stoker's *Dracula*. Though Stoker's novel was published in 1897, stories and superstitions of vampires existed long before his birth. No one can say for certain when the first vampire story was told, but throughout the world, many cultures tell tales of undead or bloodthirsty creatures.

These savage creatures can be found in the superstitions and legends of Japan, China, India, Indonesia, the Americas, Europe, Greece, and Eastern Europe to name a few locations. There are several bloodthirsty savages in Japan: a *gaki* is a pale corpse that howls for blood; a *hannya* is a beautiful woman possessed by a demon who drinks blood and eats children; *kasha* are demons that eat corpses and drink their blood. In China, a person who died by drowning, suicide, smothering, or hanging could be reanimated as a *jiang shi* (also spelled *chiang shih*), an extremely vicious revenant with pale

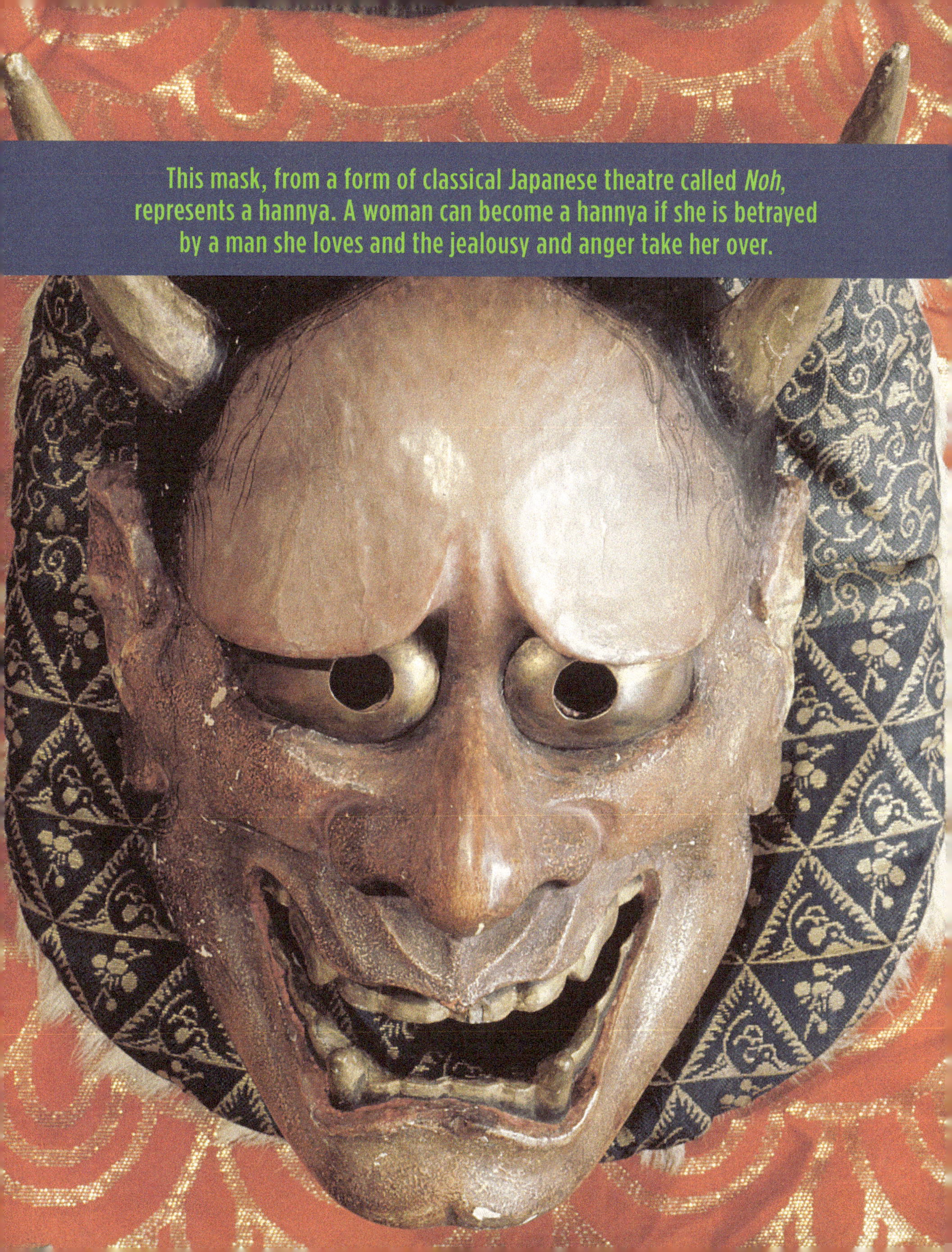

This mask, from a form of classical Japanese theatre called *Noh*, represents a hannya. A woman can become a hannya if she is betrayed by a man she loves and the jealousy and anger take her over.

skin and long, sharp fingernails who would rip body parts from its prey and drain their life force. Garlic, salt, and metal filings were used to repel a jiang shi. Thunder is one of the things that could kill them. In India, Hindu mythology tells of demons called *rakshasas* that had a taste for carnage, and the lower ranked *hatu-dhanas* that fed on the human remains left by the rakshasas. Indonesia's bloodthirsty beast, the *penanggalan,* is described as a midwife by day who has made a pact with the devil. At night she becomes a flying, bloody, detached head that wails and searches for women in labor to lap up the blood of childbirth. There is even a vampire in Greek mythology! A young man named Ambrogio fell in love with a woman Apollo (the sun god) wanted for his own. Apollo caused the young man's skin to burn when exposed to the sun as punishment. Ambrogio then went to Hades, god of the underworld, for

This portrait of Vlad Dracula dates to about 1450. "Dracula" is Romanian for "dragon" and "devil." Vlad's father belonged to the Order of the Dragon, a secret brotherhood of knights.

help. He next sought help from Artemis, goddess of the hunt, and stole her silver bow for Hades. Artemis made silver burn his skin. Later, taking pity on the lovelorn lad, she gave him immortality, super strength, and fangs so he could kill animals. He was to use their blood to write love poems to Selena (his love).

The legends of vampires from Eastern Europe may be based on a count, born in Transylvania, Romania. His name was Vlad Dracula and he ruled Walachia, Romania, intermittently from 1456 to 1462. He was not a vampire, but he was a ruthlessly cruel ruler who fought off the Ottoman Empire. He was nicknamed Vlad the Impaler because he liked to kill his enemies by impaling them on wooden stakes. Rumor has it that he liked to have his impaled victims around when he dined so he could dip his bread into their blood. *Dracula* expert Elizabeth Miller maintains that Bram Stoker did not base his novel on Vlad Dracula, though there are some strong similarities.

All of these legends and tales greatly influenced the vampire stories told throughout American history. They continue to have an effect on vampire books, movies, and more today!

1

THE ORIGINS OF VAMPIRE LEGENDS IN AMERICA

In the United States, vampire books, movies, and television shows have become increasingly popular. How did it all start? What experiences did people have here in the early days of the colonies to spread the fear and superstition of vampires? What experiences did the colonists have in their homelands that led them to import these beliefs? There were no movies or TV shows and few books. Most early settlers came from Europe and brought the stories with them.

VAMPIRE MANIA SWEEPS THROUGH EUROPE

Vampire myths became real to the people of the Middle Ages (fifth to fourteenth centuries CE) in Europe, as plagues in the fourteenth century wiped out entire villages. As members of a family succumbed to the illness, they were often left with bloody lesions around the mouth. Suspicions arose that one member was undead and killing the others. Commonly, anyone with an unusual illness was labeled a vampire. Sometimes their bodies were exhumed to look for signs of vampirism. A body buried in an above ground vault in winter could look very fresh several weeks later. To prevent him or her from rising again in the night, a wooden stake would be driven into the heart, or the heart would be removed and burned. Some corpses were decapitated and burned, even into the nineteenth century.

From the late seventeenth century on, vampire mania gradually swept Europe. The vampire superstitions in then-exotic Eastern Europe filtered back to the West and caused a sensation, inspiring authors to write books and plays about vampires. In the Romantic era of the nineteenth century—an era obsessed with superstitions, irrational emotions, and the supernatural—vampires captured the popular imagination.

VAMPIRE STORIES CROSS THE ATLANTIC OCEAN

When the colonies were established in America, vampires were already firmly rooted in European popular culture. The European

This painting by an unknown artist shows Saint Francois praying over plague victims in medieval France. Fear, death, and religion all fed into vampire lore.

settlers who spread across North America brought two types of vampire knowledge with them: images of the vampires they had seen onstage and read about in books; and the ancient folk beliefs of their ancestors, which they carried in their collective memory.

New England was one of the first regions in North America to be colonized. Among the first settlers were the Puritans, passionate Protestants dedicated to stripping all Catholic vestiges from their faith and creating a "pure" new Christianity. Despite, or maybe because of, the early settlers' zeal, New England has always been vulnerable to superstitions and spiritual fads.

During the famous Salem witch trials of 1692, hundreds of men and women in Massachusetts were accused of witchcraft, nineteen were convicted and hanged, and one man was crushed to death. In the late nineteenth century, the spiritualism movement spread rapidly through the region. For a time, many New Englanders believed it was possible to communicate with the spirit world through séances, special meetings for consulting with the dead.

THE NEW ENGLAND VAMPIRE PANIC

It was only scarcely more than a hundred years after the Salem witch trials that New England again was in a panic about strange behavior and unexplained deaths. Before modern medicine, a common cause of death in New England was tuberculosis, an infectious disease that primarily affects the lungs and can be fatal. Symptoms include weight loss, fever, and punishing, bloody coughs. When tubercular people cough or sneeze, they spread their bacterial infection through the air. Today, many Americans are protected against tuberculosis by immunization, and the active disease can be treated with antibiotics.

Tuberculosis was once called "consumption" because the infected wasted away as if consumed from within. People didn't know what caused consumption, and they didn't know how to cure it, so they turned to traditional folk beliefs. In New England, when multiple people in one family died from consumption, the first person to die was believed to have become a vampire that returned from the grave to drain blood and vitality from his or her kin. History records the details of some of these creepy cases.

In his book *Vampires, Burial, and Death*, scholar Paul Barber attempts to explain Eastern European vampire folklore by examining the natural process of decomposition. Barber points out that some corpses decay faster than others. A body laid to rest in the cold winter ground will remain better preserved than a body buried in high summer. Superstitious folk digging up a body buried in winter might have been surprised by how healthy it looked. A dead body's skin naturally recedes, creating the illusion that the teeth, nails, and hair have grown. But how can one explain reports of vampire corpses swollen with blood, with red cheeks and bloody mouths? Barber explains that after death, corpses swell with natural gases. The increased pressure inside the body can push blood out of the nose and mouth. The corpse then appears engorged with blood.

As the vampire scare continued, neighbors insisted that bodies be exhumed to discover who was the vampire. They used various

This seven-hundred-year-old skeleton was discovered in Sozopol, Bulgaria, in 2012. To prevent the man from coming back as a vampire, his remains had been pinned down by an iron rod through the chest, and his teeth had been pulled before being buried.

methods to keep the vampire from rising again: a stake through the heart, removal and burning of the heart, or decapitation.

OTHER SUSPECTED VAMPIRES IN NEW ENGLAND

There are several documented cases of suspected vampires in New England, most likely due to tuberculosis outbreaks. Sarah Tillinghast

NEW ENGLAND'S MOST FAMOUS VAMPIRE

The most famous New England "vampire" was Mercy Brown, from Exeter, Rhode Island. In late 1883, her mother, Mary, died of consumption quickly, followed by Mercy's eldest sister, Olive. Nineteen-year-old Mercy died in 1892, and then her brother became sick. Their father, George, decided one of the women must be a vampire. When they were disinterred (dug up), Mary and Olive were rotted away, but Mercy's body lay on its side and she seemed barely decomposed. Her heart appeared to contain fresh liquid blood. Along with her liver, the heart was burned. Their doctor recommended the sick brother drink the ashes as medicine. Two months later, he died. Mercy's grave exists to this day and is visited regularly.

of Exeter, Rhode Island, the eldest of fourteen children, became ill and died in 1799. After six of her siblings died, her mother began to complain of losing energy and having terrible dreams of Sarah visiting her at night. Neighbors decided to exhume the children and found Sarah's body suspiciously well preserved. They removed all the children's hearts and burned them. Only one more Tillinghast child died after that.

Nancy Young from Foster, Rhode Island, died of consumption in 1827 at age nineteen. As with Sarah, several of her siblings began to weaken and fade. Her father, Levi, had Nancy exhumed and burned and directed his children to breathe in the ashes. Unfortunately, five more of Nancy's siblings died anyway.

BELIEVE IN VAMPIRES.

Rhode Islanders Who Are Sure That They Do Exist.

Instances Told of Where the Living Have Been Attacked and Preyed Upon by These Representatives of an Unseen World.

A MEMBER OF THE ANTI-VAMPIRE PARTY.

This editorial cartoon from the January 27, 1896 edition of the *Boston Daily Globe* accompanied an article on the superstitions of rural Rhode Island.

A family in Jewett City, Connecticut, the Rays, were struck by a now familiar disaster. Within ten years, the father, Lemuel, and two sons passed away. When a third son, named Henry, became sick, the community decided to exhume the three previously deceased Rays and burned them. The third son, Henry, died anyway.

2

MULTICULTURAL VAMPIRE LEGENDS IN AMERICA

Almost every culture has myths of some type of blood-sucking undead beast. Exploring some of these myths will show the differences and similarities in their cultural experiences, perhaps shedding light on their underlying belief systems. In Mexico and Guatemala, the native peoples were vastly influenced by the Spaniards who came looking for gold and to bring Christianity to them (and everyone else in the Caribbean and South and Latin America). Louisiana was more influenced by the French and the Cajun peoples who, originally from France, were forced to move from Canada, so their myths may be a bit different. Then there are the Native Americans who had their own sets of beliefs long before European settlers came on the scene.

VAMPIRIC CREATURES FROM MEXICO AND GUATEMALA

Described as a friendly vampire who can become extremely vicious when upset, the *chorti* are wild men who live deep in forests and caves in Guatemala and Mexico. They are nature lovers and described as big and hairy with their feet on backwards. They have steel claws and can slice a man's head off and feed till there are only bones left.

Bound to Aztec gods, the *civatateo* is a Mexican vampire witch who prefers to attack young children. She is believed to have been a noblewoman who died in childbirth. If she has children as a civitateo, they will be born vampires. She paints her arms white and wears tattered clothing.

Tlaciques, of the Nahuatl Indians in Mexico, is believed to be a vampire that can turn into a ball of flame or a turkey. During either state, it can feed without anyone knowing.

One last intriguing case was supposedly discovered when a government worker questioned a strange phrase on the "cause of death" line on many death certificates, most of them infants: *"chupado por la bruja"* which means "sucked by a witch." An investigation was launched and a law passed that required all cases with this cause of death be referred to state medical authorities. This all happened in a small state east of Mexico City. The locals,

HOW TO SPOT A VAMPIRE

With so many vampire stories and legends out there, each with their own special gifts and limitations, it can get pretty confusing, except for the trait that they all drink blood. In the earliest vampire tales, a vampire's reflection would not show up in a mirror, they did not cast a shadow, sunlight would burn them up, silver would hurt them, and they spent their days in coffins. They usually have super strength and speed. Some can fly or turn into bats. Vampires are immortal unless staked or burned in sunlight. There are other variations depending on what the author needs the vampire to do. Bram Stoker's Count Dracula could go out during the day, and some vampires have special rings that protect them from the sun. Though vampires need to drink blood, some of them also eat food, although they don't need it. They can also use mind control to lure their prey into a secluded spot for a bite.

A vampire bat hangs out on the wall of a cave. As their name suggests, vampire bats feed on blood from animals.

retaining their pre-conquest beliefs, still spoke Nahuatl and shared many Aztec beliefs. One ancient belief they kept to themselves was belief in the *tlahuelpuchi*, a female vampire who could shape-shift and feed on the lives of infants. This creature dates back thousands of years. They live as humans with families during the day. And they are not made; they are born this way, although no one would ever know until the girl reaches puberty. At that time, she suddenly knows and her soul leaves her for three days. There is nothing to be done about it, so even if the family knows about it, they tell no one. She must kill a baby once a month and must prepare for it with a ritual in which she removes her legs and leaves them at home. When she turns herself into an animal, she becomes luminescent.

NATIVE AMERICAN VAMPIRE MYTHS

Various Native American peoples have legends about immortal dead humans that prey on living humans. Northern Algonquian tribes avoid the windigos (*chenoo* in the Micmac language and *giwakwa* in the Abenaki language) who are cannibal ice giants. The legend goes that they were human once, but they committed some unspeakable crime, such as cannibalism. This turns their hearts to ice. Sometimes an evil wizard is involved in the transformation. They are then fated to roam the wilderness savagely consuming every human they meet until they are killed.

The Navajo have their skin-walkers. In this legend as in the previous one, skin-walkers are created when a human commits some terrible crime or sin, such as using forbidden magic or killing a parent. They are able to shape-shift into animals and hunt humans at night. They resemble vampires in that they devour humans, avoid sunlight, and can use mind control to gain power over their prey. Skin-walkers return to human form during the day. To kill a skin-walker, it is best to find out his human identity and go after him when he is vulnerable during the day.

Many tribes share the folklore about the Mosquito Man, a man-eating monster who sticks his long snout into a person's head and sucks out their brains. He is so sneaky that people around do not even know anything has happened. The Haidas have a common story in which people at a party were passing a new baby around while Mosquito Man stealthily sucked out its brain and passed it on to the next person who was sickened to find what had happened. Finally, a man tricks the monster and kills it, burning its body. The monster swears that he will never stop eating human flesh; the ashes that rise up from the beast's burning body become mosquitoes.

The windigo's appearance varies depending on the particular Native American nation the legend is from. But across cultures, the windigo represents evil, especially greed and bloodthirst.

The Wabanaki tribes of New England feared *skadegamutc*.

These were ghost-witches who were usually created by the death of an evil sorcerer. The sorcerer would then rise from the dead at night to kill and devour humans. He appeared to be a regular corpse in daylight hours and could only be killed forever by fire.

Another Native American undead creature, similar to the Indonesian penanggalan (a screaming, rolling, flying head by night), Rolling Head, is the Iroquois monster created when a woman is unfaithful and is killed by her husband. She comes back as a reanimated, disembodied head that flies or rolls around to seek revenge on her husband.

A REAL VAMPIRE IN NEW ORLEANS

Maybe it's because of the book and movie series by Anne Rice, or the fact that New Orleans is a melting pot of supernatural beliefs, but of all the cities of the Old South, New Orleans has a particularly haunted history. Founded by the French, the city was also once ruled by the Spanish and has been influenced heavily by the Creoles (the descendants of French and Spanish colonials), African slaves, and Irish and German immigrants. The city has a unique spiritual profile, a rich gumbo of European, Native American, and African religious, spiritual, and superstitious folk beliefs.

According to local tales, a mysterious man arrived in New Orleans in the early 1900s. He was wealthy, elegant, sophisticated, and threw extravagant dinner parties. His name was Jacques St. Germain. He quickly became a hit in New Orleans society. Though he served lavish dinners, he never partook of any of the

New Orleans capitalizes on its spooky reputation by giving ghost and vampire walking tours in the French Quarter.

food himself. He simply drank from a silver chalice what everyone assumed was wine.

His guests loved to hear him speak, they loved his accent and he told the most amusing stories of France, Italy, and other countries. He claimed to be a direct descendent of Comte (Count) de St. Germain, a close friend and servant of King Louis XV in the eighteenth century. His guests were skeptical but could not deny his uncanny resemblance to the count. Jacques was about forty years old, the same age as the count in his portraits. He related tales of the count, King Louis XV, and France with such detail it seemed as if he'd been there himself. While entertained and amused, his guests began to wonder, could he be the Comte de St. Germain, having found some way to stay young all this time? Jacques appeared to enjoy the mystery surrounding him.

One night, disaster struck. A young woman jumped from a second-floor balcony of his house. She was hysterical, and the guests helping her called the police. She finally managed to utter that Jacques had tried to bite her neck. As she was taken to the hospital, the police told St. Germain they would not disturb him this late at night and asked him to stop by the station in the morning. Jacques never showed up that morning. When the police went to his house, he had disappeared, leaving most of his belongings behind. In his bedroom the police found, the rumor describes, several uncorked wine bottles that contained a mixture of blood and wine!

3

VAMPIRES BEGIN TO EVOLVE INTO FICTION

As science advanced and free public education was instituted, vampire legends generally fell into just that category: legend. Vampires were no longer thought to be real as more scientific explanations for unexplained events became known. Increased knowledge about and more effective diagnoses and treatment for tuberculosis put to rest those specific vampire fears. As medicine evolved to establish more accurate ways to determine if someone was dead and mortuary practices improved so no one was in danger of waking up in a coffin underground, many fears of the undead disappeared. The term "saved by the bell" originated from a fear of being buried alive. Coffins would be constructed with a rope inside attached to a bell above ground. If someone awoke in a coffin (and they really did), they could pull the rope. When people heard the bell ringing, they would immediately dig up the prematurely buried person.

A SCARY GOOD TIME

Since the nineteenth century, vampires have been popular subjects in literature. First, John Polidori, personal doctor to the famous British poet Lord Byron, wrote *The Vampire* (1819). It was based on a story by Lord Byron and starred an aristocratic and demonic vampire who reminded many people of Lord Byron.

The serialized novel *Varney the Vampire; Or, the Feast of Blood* was written in Britain in the mid-1840s as a series of cheap pamphlets known as penny dreadfuls. When the entire work was published, it included more than two hundred twenty chapters! Also, in the 1840s, Edgar Allen Poe, the American master of the macabre, wrote several short stories about the dead returning from the grave to prey upon the living. The novel *Carmilla* by Irish author Joseph Sheridan Le Fanu, published in 1872, featured a mysterious but beautiful woman preying on a lovely girl.

But the vampire novel that truly captured the world's imagination was *Dracula* by Irish journalist, theater critic, and stage manager Bram Stoker. The character Dracula was the template of the classic Hollywood vampire: a haughty, imperious count who seduced his victims and then held them in his thrall.

Since the publication of Stoker's novel, stage and screen adaptations have condensed, twisted, and transformed the original story. Still, the plot of *Dracula* is familiar to people today: lawyer Jonathan

This is the cover from one of the original *Varney the Vampire* publications.

Harker travels to Castle Dracula in Transylvania on a business trip and meets the count himself. In the second half of the book, Dracula moves to London, where he fixates on Harker's fiancée, Mina, and her friend, Lucy. The count also earns a fan—a mental patient named Renfield who eats insects. He reveres Dracula as a master of sucking others' life force.

When Lucy wastes away, Professor Abraham van Helsing realizes she has become a vampire and stakes her through the heart. Next, Dracula feeds off Mina, and she, too, slowly falls under his spell. Luckily, Dr. Van Helsing, Harker, and their friends use the connection between Mina and Dracula to defeat the fiend. In the end, the entire group follows Dracula back to Transylvania, and they finally kill him.

In 1954, Richard Matheson published *I Am Legend,* which was one of the first to combine zombies and vampires for a new genre of science fiction. The highly prolific writer, Stephen King wrote *Salem's Lot*, his second published novel, in 1975, in which a writer goes back to a town he lived in as a child only to find that the townspeople are becoming vampires. Next came Anne Rice in 1976 with her debut novel *Interview with the Vampire,* which launched a series of vampire novels. It also seems to have begun the popularity of vampire novel series, especially for young adults.

VAMPIRES ON THE BIG SCREEN

It was inevitable that the popularity of vampire novels and folklore would soon expand to the earliest motion pictures. People were already intrigued by the idea of watching moving pictures on a big screen. Movies quickly became a popular form of entertainment, especially for the average working person who could not afford to attend live plays or the opera. Vampires were delightfully scary in a darkened movie theater.

Since the early days of silent film, vampires have stalked the silver screen. In 1896, the French movie *Le Manoir du Diable* (*The House of the Devil* in its US release) was just three minutes long. It featured a sorcerer who transformed into a giant bat.

Around the globe, movies based on vampires became popular. Successful films included *The Vampire* in 1910, the Italian *Tower of the Vampire* in 1913, the 1920 Russian *Dracula*, and the 1921 Hungarian *Drakula*.

REAL-LIFE VAMPIRE TRIBES

John Edgar Browning from the Georgia Institute of Technology has been conducting studies of real vampires living in New Orleans and Buffalo, New York. They use the term "Real Vampires" to identify themselves. They are not immortal and cannot turn into bats, but many have had fangs installed and many live a nocturnal lifestyle. They need blood or psychic energy from donors to feel healthy and feed only on willing donors. They believe their nature (the need for blood or psychic energy) becomes apparent around puberty and that it is caused by a lack of subtle energies in their own bodies. The ones Browning has interviewed come from all walks of life, are aged from eighteen to fifty, and often live together as a family or tribe. Most surprising, they do not seem to know much about vampires in popular culture.

One of the spookiest early vampire films was *Nosferatu* (1922) by German filmmaker F. W. Murnau. The film was a close adaptation of Stoker's novel *Dracula*, but the title and character names were changed to avoid copyright infringement. (Florence Stoker, the author's widow, sued the filmmaker anyway.) *Nosferatu* is an expressionistic movie, full of horrific images and dramatic special effects. Vampire Count Orlok is closely modeled on ancient folkloric vampires: He is bald, with a twisted face, creepily long fingernails, and fangs.

Perhaps the most famous vampire movie is *Dracula* (1931). Based on the 1924 hit stage play, the movie was a "talkie," one of the earliest films with dialogue and a soundtrack. The star of both the play and film, Hungarian actor Bela Lugosi (1882–1956), would become the most iconic Dracula in history. Lugosi, with his dark hair, sharp nose, long black cape, and thick accent, would forever be identified with the Transylvanian count.

THE VAMPIRE CHANGES WITH THE TIMES

In the war-torn world of the 1930s and 1940s, escapist entertainment became an important part of survival in the midst of the horrors of losing men in battle and women working full-time in the war effort. During this time, vampire movies were released nearly every year. At first, there were sequels and spin-offs and later on, spoofs, parodies, and satires. The vampire movies changed to reflect the hopes and fears of each new era.

In the mid-1950s, America was engaged in a space race with its rival, the Soviet Union. The national obsession with outer space was

Bela Lugosi was born near the western border of Transylvania, not far from where Bram Stoker set Count Dracula's castle in the Carpathian Mountains.

reflected in a crop of vampire science-fiction movies such as *Not of This Earth* (1957), *It! The Vampire from Beyond Space* (1958), *First Man into Space* (1959), and the legendary cult classic *Plan 9 from Outer Space* (1959).

Wesley Snipe's Blade character could be taken for any other run-of-the-mill leather-clad, weapon-wielding superhero . . . except for his unearthly gold eyes, sharp fangs, and need for blood to stay alive.

In the 1960s and 1970s, London's Hammer Studios made brightly colored, sensational, and shocking vampire movies that were full of blood and gore. Christopher Lee, the studio's Dracula, and Peter Cushing, as Van Helsing, became legendary. The pair starred in movies such as *Horror of Dracula* (1958), *The Brides of Dracula* (1960), *Dracula: Prince of Darkness* (1966), *Dracula Has Risen from the Grave* (1968), and *Dracula A.D. 1972* (1972). Their work had a huge influence on the American work produced in Hollywood.

From 1966 to 1971, the first important vampire character appeared on television: Barnabas Collins, the vampire star of ABC's gothic soap opera *Dark Shadows*. Actor Jonathan Frid played the vampire.

The cultural trends of the 1980s were reflected in that decade's vampires. Rock star David Bowie costarred in the gothic classic *The Hunger* in 1983. Vampires even found their way into the celebrated teen movies of the 1980s: *The Lost Boys* (1987) presented a gang of teenage vampires living in California.

In the 1990s, Francis Ford Coppola brought Bram Stoker's original story to life in vivid images in *Bram Stoker's Dracula* (1992). In *Blade* (1998), Wesley Snipes played a half-vampire vampire hunter (based on a popular Marvel comic book character) working to make the world safe for humans. At the start of the new millennium, the action movie *Underworld* (2003) and its sequels were set in a dark world with vampires and werewolves battling for supremacy.

4

VAMPIRES UNLEASH A WEALTH OF POPULAR ENTERTAINMENT

No longer a source of fear and loss, vampire legends have inspired innumerable books, movies, games, and options for the imagination. The only traits that seem to be consistent among various treatments are the drinking of blood and immortality. Otherwise, some are good, some are bad, some are sensitive to sunlight, some sparkle in the sun, some can shape-shift, some cannot, some can fly or turn into bats, and on and on. Their immortality makes them perfect characters in historical novels since they can exist from ancient Greece and before, right up to modern times. They are also well traveled. Anything a writer's imagination can come up with will work in a vampire novel.

MODERN VAMPIRE NOVELS, MOVIES, AND TV SHOWS

Anne Rice is a native of New Orleans, and her novels often linger in that city. Her first book *Interview with the Vampire* became the most popular and influential vampire book since *Dracula*. Its success led to a beloved series of more than twelve novels.

Some of her vampires are globetrotters that have spent time in Eastern Europe; England; France; ancient Egypt; Constantinople;

Tom Cruise portrays the vampire Lestat in *Interview with the Vampire*.

Venice; San Francisco; Washington, DC; and other locales. Rice's vampires are glamorous, artistic, and emotional, and they fall in love easily. Many traditional vampire rules don't apply to them. For instance, they can safely look at a cross, and they can't be killed with a stake through the heart. Some have magical powers. They do need to drink blood, however, and sunlight can kill those vampires who are still relatively young—say, less than a thousand years old.

So far, the Anne Rice books have spawned two movies: *Interview with the Vampire* (1994) with Tom Cruise, Brad Pitt, and Kirsten Dunst, and *The Queen of the Damned* (2002), starring the late singer Aaliyah.

The *Twilight* series is one of the most phenomenally successful young adult book series ever. In the first book, *Twilight* (2005), heroine Bella Swan moves from sunny Phoenix to perpetually foggy Forks, Washington, to live with her father. There, she meets and falls in love with an impossibly handsome vampire named Edward Cullen. Edward looks like a teenager, but he is actually 104 years old. He survives on animal, instead of human, blood. When another vampire threatens Bella, Edward and his family struggle to protect her. Sequels include *New Moon* (2006), *Eclipse* (2007), and *Breaking Dawn* (2008). Eventually, Bella faces a choice between Edward and close friend and rival love interest Jacob, who just happens to be a werewolf.

The book series was adapted into several incredibly successful movies, starring Kristen Stewart and Robert Pattinson. The *Twilight*

Edward and Bella, played by Robert Pattinson and Kristen Stewart, share a romantic moment in this scene from *Twilight*.

novels and movies became so popular that the real-life town of Forks, Washington, is now a tourist destination.

Author Chelsea Quinn Yarbro created a series about an immortal vampire named Count Saint-Germain, based on a historical count rumored to be an alchemist. According to Jacques Casanova's memoirs, the count claimed to be three hundred years old.

In Yarbro's books, Saint-Germain is a vampire. The continuing series follows his adventures through history: He spends time in medieval Florence, ancient Rome, the Old West, Moorish Spain, and many other places. Saint-Germain is a good vampire who tries to use his powers to help people. Unlike other vampires, he prefers to take small amounts of blood from willing victims. Interestingly, Saint-Germain does not sleep in a coffin. In order to rest on native soil, he has special compartments built into his shoes and the foundations of his houses.

The *Southern Vampire Mysteries* by Charlaine Harris are set in a world where vampires coexist with humans. In the first book, *Dead Until Dark* (2001), the Japanese invention of synthetic blood has made it possible for vampires to "come out of the coffin" and make their identities public. However, vampires face human prejudice—and some refuse to give up hunting. What's more, vampires are in danger because their blood has magical properties when ingested by humans.

In 2008, the book series was adapted into a hit HBO show for adults called *True Blood*, with Anna Paquin as psychic barmaid Sookie Stackhouse and Stephen Moyer as her vampire boyfriend, Bill Compton. The show ran for seven seasons and garnered numerous awards, including a Golden Globe and an Emmy.

L. J. Smith's *Vampire Diaries* series tells the story of teen Elena Gilbert, who must choose between two vampire brothers competing for her affection. There are several related book series: *The Return* series, *The Hunters* series, and *Stefan's Diaries*. In 2009, *The Vampire Diaries* became a TV series on the CW television network, starring Nina Dobrev, Paul Wesley, and Ian

Somerhalder. It was popular with teen audiences and ran for eight seasons. It now has spawned two spin-offs: *The Originals* and *Legacies.*

(From left to right) Paul Wesley, Nina Dobrev, and Ian Somerhalder battle evil forces, both out in the world and within themselves, in *The Vampire Diaries.*

Vampires have played an important role in television shows and movies, as well as books. First, in the movie *Buffy the Vampire Slayer* (1992), a Southern California cheerleader learns that she has been chosen by fate to slay vampires. Following the movie's success, screenwriter and filmmaker Joss Whedon created the long-running TV series *Buffy the Vampire Slayer* starring Sarah Michelle Gellar. In turn, the show led to novelizations, comic books, video games, and a popular spin-off TV series called *Angel*. The "Buffy-verse" is full of demons, robots, witches, warlocks, and other marvelous beings. It's a world with complex and nuanced storylines that sometimes spin out in different directions. There are few series that have had more devoted and active fans.

THE GOTH SUBCULTURE

The Gothic novels of the Romantic era were set in ruined medieval churches and graveyards, often featured vampires and ghosts, and revolved around dark secrets and morbid obsessions. Hundreds of years later, many of today's teens are drawn to this dark world. They express their interest in the dark, the morbid, and the supernatural by becoming "Goths."

The first song in the music genre that came to be known as gothic rock was Bauhaus's "Bela Lugosi's Dead" (1979). Bauhaus's fellow bands Siouxsie and the Banshees and the Damned also played moody post-punk and dressed in black with dramatic makeup. However, none of these early bands actually called themselves goth. As time went on, their fans forged a subculture inspired by Gothic novels, horror movies,

There are many different styles within the Goth subculture. Perhaps the one most closely associated with vampires is the Victorian Goth look, which features long skirts, corsets, and bell sleeves for women.

vampire lore, the occult, and the Victorian era. Later goth bands include Sisters of Mercy, Rosetta Stone, and Marilyn Manson.

Because Goths are gloomy and fascinated with death, they are often misunderstood as advocating violence or satanism (devil worship). In reality, Goths are usually tolerant, nonviolent, creative, and compassionate. They tend to favor black clothing, dark hair and makeup, punk gear including piercings, and medieval-inspired clothing elements such as corsets and velvet skirts. Goths gravitate toward the literary works of Edgar Allen Poe, H. P. Lovecraft, and Anne Rice. Filmmaker Tim Burton has made many classic goth movies, including *Edward Scissorhands* and *The Nightmare Before Christmas*.

Many Goths love vampires so much that they dress in Dracula-inspired gear, use makeup to make their skin paler, or even wear false vampire teeth!

VIDEO GAMES AND MORE

Vampires have also infested the gaming world, in video games such as the *Bloodrayne* series and the *Castlevania* series. For those who would rather play with dice than electronics, there are role-playing games such as *Vampire: The Masquerade*, *Vampire: The Masquerade—Bloodlines*, and *Vampire: The Requiem*.

Not even children are safe from vampires. In the *Bunnicula* books by James Howe, a family takes home a vampire bunny. The popular and long-running children's TV show *Sesame Street* features a Dracula-like character named the Count, who loves to—what else?—count. There is even a popular chocolate-flavored cereal called Count Chocula!

THE VAMPIRE AS A SYMBOL

Over the years, vampires have undergone an incredible transformation. In centuries past, vampires were mindless corpses rotting in their graves that rose to suck the blood of the living. These vampires symbolized the forces humans cannot control in nature.

Today's vampires are seductive, beautiful, and immortal. They are often loners who long to join human society but are exiled from it. Many are fundamentally good and struggle to suppress their lethal urges. They symbolize the forces people cannot control in themselves.

Modern vampires have gone from monsters to romantic heroes, from dead to immortal. Why?

In her book *Our Vampires, Ourselves*, Nina Auerbach theorizes that in every era of history, people create a new type of vampire to embody their hopes and fears. Maybe the same is true of every storyteller—including every novelist, TV producer, and movie director. For example, *Twilight* created a relationship between a girl and a vampire that demonstrates how teenage girls might both long for romance and still fear it.

How will vampire stories develop in the future? Only one thing is certain: As society changes, vampire legends will continue to evolve.

BIBLIOGRAPHY

Animal Planet. "Lost Tapes: Skinwalker, Navajo Shapeshifter: Animal Planet." 2011. Retrieved April 9, 2011 (http://animal.discovery.com/tv/lost-tapes/skinwalker).

Auerbach, Nina. *Our Vampires, Ourselves*. Chicago, IL: University of Chicago Press, 1995.

Barber, Paul. *Vampires, Burial, and Death: Folklore and Reality*. New ed. New Haven, CT: Yale University Press, 2010.

Bibeau, Paul. *Sundays with Vlad: From Pennsylvania to Transylvania, One Man's Quest to Live in the World of the Undead*. New York, NY: Three Rivers Press, 2007.

Browning, John Edgar. "The Real Vampires of New Orleans and Buffalo: A Research Note Towards Comparative Ethnography." Georgia Institute of Technology, *Palgrave Communications*, Vol. 1, pp. 15006. 2015.

FirstPeople.us. "Native American Legends: The Cannibal Who Was Burned: Haida." Retrieved April 7, 2011 (http://www.firstpeople.us/FP-Html-Legends/TheCannibalWhoWasBurned-Haida.html).

FirstPeople.us. "Native American Legends: How Mosquitoes Came to Be: Tlingit." Retrieved April 7, 2011 (http://www.firstpeople.us/FP-Html-Legends/How_Mosquitoes_Came_To_Be-Tlingit.html).

Jenkins, Mark. *Vampire Forensics: Uncovering the Origins of an Enduring Legend*. Washington, DC: National Geographic, 2010.

Karg, Barbara, Arjean Spaite, and Rick Sutherland. *The Everything Vampire Book: From Vlad the Impaler to the Vampire Lestat—A History of Vampires in Literature, Film, and Legend.* Avon, MA: Adams Media, 2009.

Kelleher, Colm, and George Knapp. "Skinwalkers—What Are They?" Rense.com. Retrieved April 9, 2011 (http://www.rense.com/general77/skin.htm).

MacDougal, Shane. *The Vampire Slayers' Field Guide to the Undead.* Huntingdon Valley, PA: Strider Nolan Publishing, 2003.

Maine Folklife Center, The University of Maine. "Northeast Folklore—Miscellaneous Malecite Tales." Retrieved April 7, 2011 (http://umaine.edu/folklife/publications/online-publications/northeast-folklore/miscellaneous-malecite-tales).

Melton, J. Gordon. *The Vampire Book: The Encyclopedia of the Undead.* 3rd ed. Canton, MI: Visible Ink Press, 2011.

"Native American Vampires of Myth and Legend." Native Languages of the Americas. Retrieved February 27, 2019 (http://www.native-languages.org/native-vampires.htm).

Taylor, Troy. "Haunted New Orleans History." 2000. Retrieved April 7, 2011 (http://www.prairieghosts.com/nohistory3.html).

GLOSSARY

carnage Great destruction of life.

consumption An outdated name for pulmonary tuberculosis (TB). TB was once called consumption because victims looked as if they were being consumed, or eaten up, from the inside.

corpse A dead human body.

decomposition The process a dead plant, animal, or human undergoes as it is naturally broken down; the act of rotting.

exhume To dig up a dead body from its grave.

expressionistic Having to do with a movement in the arts that emphasized expression of the artist's inner experiences.

iconic Characterized by fame; being a widely known symbol.

impale To pierce with a long and sharp stick, spear, pole, or stake.

lesion Damage to a body part because of injury or disease.

occult Having to do with the supernatural, magical, or esoteric.

reanimated Returning to life from death.

revenant Someone or something that returns from the dead.

spiritualism A belief that spirits can communicate with the living.

supernatural Describes something that cannot be explained by science.

superstition A belief or fear based on tradition or irrational thought, rather than science, reason, or experience.

tuberculosis An infectious disease caused by bacteria. It often infects the lungs and can cause fever, weight loss, bloody coughs, difficulty breathing, fever, chest pain, and other symptoms.

FURTHER READING

BOOKS

Netzley, Patricia D. *Do Vampires Exist?* San Diego, CA: ReferencePoint Press, Inc., 2016.

Niver, Heather Moor. *Was Count Dracula Real?* New York, NY: Enslow Publishing, 2018.

Stoker, Bram. *Dracula*. Newbury, Berkshire, UK: Baker Street Press, 2018.

White, Steve. *Hunting Vampires.* New York, NY: Rosen Young Adult, 2017.

WEBSITES

Ancient Origins: Vampires

www.ancient-origins.net/searchall/vampires

Read articles about vampire lore from around the world.

History Channel: Vampire History

www.history.com/topics/folklore/vampire-history

Learn more about vampires throughout history.

Native Languages of the Americas: Native American Vampires of Myth and Legend

www.native-languages.org/native-vampires.htm

Find out more about Native American myths about vampires.

INDEX

Read More

Mara, Will. *If You Were a Kid During the Civil War.* New York: Children's Press, 2017.

Schmidt, Gary D. *So Tall Within: Sojourner Truth's Long Walk Toward Freedom.* New York: Roaring Book Press, 2018.

Troupe, Thomas Kingsley. *Harriet Tubman's Escape.* North Mankato, MN: Picture Window Books, 2017.

Internet Sites

Ducksters: Sojourner Truth
www.ducksters.com/history/civil_rights/sojourner_truth.php

History for Kids: Sojourner Truth
www.historyforkids.net/sojourner-truth.html

National Geographic: Abraham Lincoln
video.nationalgeographic.com/video/00000144-0a42-d3cb-a96c-7b4f37a90000

Index